U.S.A. TRAVEL GUIDES

LOUISIANA

BY ANN HEINRICHS • ILLUSTRATED BY MATT KANIA

The Child's World®
childsworld.com

Published by The Child's World®
1980 Lookout Drive • Mankato, MN 56003-1705
800-599-READ • www.childsworld.com

Ann Heinrichs is the author of more than 100 books for children and young adults. She has also enjoyed successful careers as a children's book editor and an advertising copywriter. Ann grew up in Fort Smith, Arkansas, and lives in Chicago, Illinois.

post card

About the Author
Ann Heinrichs

Matt Kania loves maps and, as a kid, dreamed of making them. In school he studied geography and cartography, and today he makes maps for a living. Matt's favorite thing about drawing maps is learning about the places they represent. Many of the maps he has created can be found in books, magazines, videos, Web sites, and public places.

post card

About the
Map Illustrator
Matt Kania

On the cover: You'll find many museums, shops, and restaurants in Jackson Square, New Orleans.

OUR LOUISIANA TRIP

LOUISIANA

Want to see things you've never seen before? Want to hear, smell, and taste new things? Just take a trip around Louisiana!

You'll see alligators and learn about swamp monsters. You'll eat crawfish and **gumbo**. You'll dress up like a pirate. Or maybe you'd rather dress like a carnival queen. You'll learn about great folks such as Louis Armstrong. You might even learn to dance the two-step.

Are you ready to hit the road? Then buckle up—we're on our way!

WELCOME TO
LOUISIANA

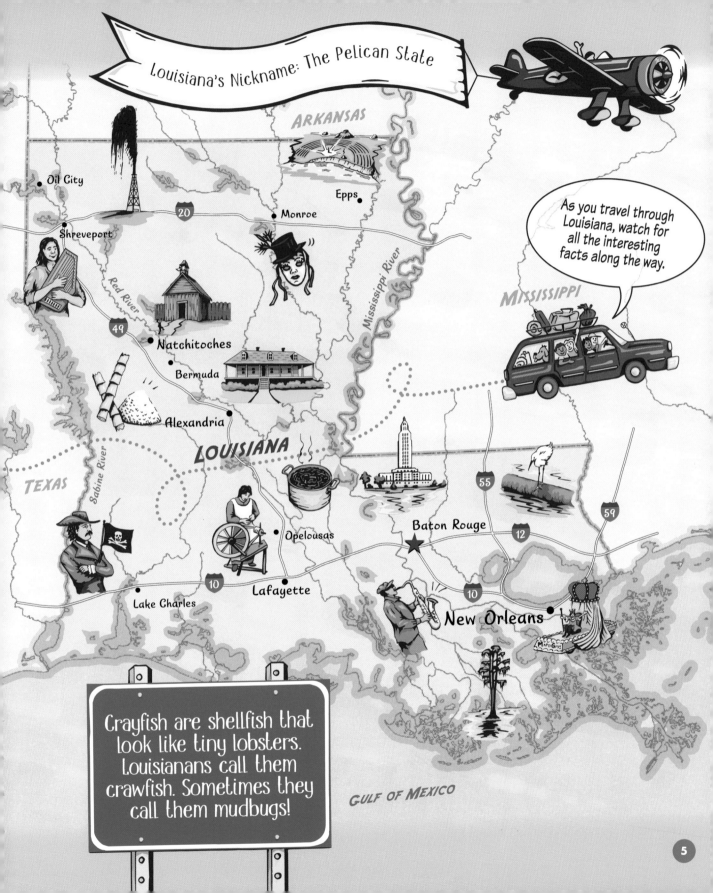

Louisiana's Nickname: The Pelican State

As you travel through Louisiana, watch for all the interesting facts along the way.

ARKANSAS

Oil City

Epps

Monroe

Shreveport

Red River

Natchitoches

Bermuda

Alexandria

LOUISIANA

TEXAS

Sabine River

Opelousas

Lafayette

Lake Charles

MISSISSIPPI

Mississippi River

Baton Rouge

New Orleans

MARDI GRAS

Crayfish are shellfish that look like tiny lobsters. Louisianans call them crawfish. Sometimes they call them mudbugs!

GULF OF MEXICO

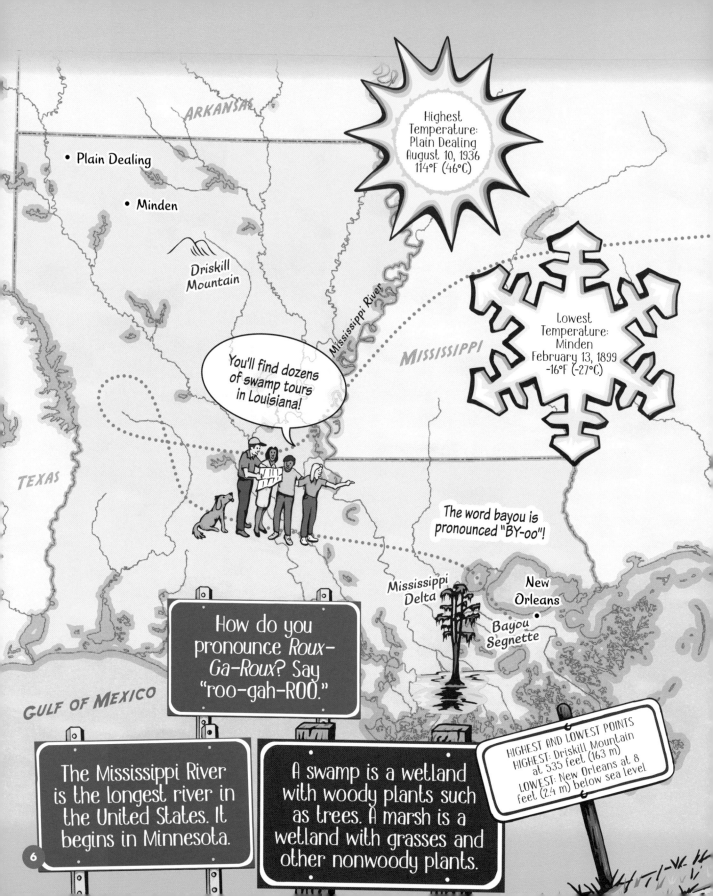

A SWAMP TOUR IN BAYOU SEGNETTE

Do you like scary stories? Then you'll love tales about the Roux-Ga-Roux. This swamp monster may sneak up and snatch you!

You can hear all about the Roux-Ga-Roux. Just take a swamp tour in Bayou Segnette.

What is a bayou? It's a slow-moving waterway. Southern Louisiana has lots of bayous. Much of this region is wet and swampy. Low, rolling hills stretch across northern Louisiana.

The Mississippi River is the state's major river. It reaches the Gulf of Mexico near New Orleans. Land near the river is called the Mississippi Delta. Soil in the Delta is very fertile. You won't find any monsters there!

You might not see the Roux-Ga-Roux, but you'll see hundreds of giant cypress trees at Bayou Segnette.

BAYOU SAUVAGE NATIONAL WILDLIFE REFUGE

You're gliding along in a boat. Tall cypress trees tower overhead. Long strands of Spanish moss are hanging down. Something long and lumpy is on the bank. Is it a log? No, it's an alligator!

You're in Bayou Sauvage near New Orleans. It's a national wildlife refuge. Louisiana's bayous and swamps are full of wildlife. Alligators, turtles, and snakes lurk in the shadows. Herons and egrets catch fish along the bank. These long-legged birds are built for wading. Minks and raccoons scurry in the leaves. They have to watch out for wildcats!

About half the state is forestland. Rabbits and deer find shelter in these forests. Even wild hogs live there.

Many birds, such as the white ibis, make their home in Bayou Sauvage National Wildlife Refuge.

Bayou Pierre Alligator Park is in Natchitoches.

STATE FLOWER
MAGNOLIA

STATE TREE
BALD CYPRESS

STATE BIRD
EASTERN BROWN PELICAN

Bayou Sauvage is French for "wild bayou."

Is that an alligator? No way. I'm sure that's a log. Okay, then you touch it!

MISSISSIPPI

Natchitoches

TEXAS

Bayou Sauvage

New Orleans

St. Charles Parish

St. Charles Parish holds an alligator festival every year. You can eat alligator sausage, alligator burgers, and fried alligator!

Louisiana is called the Pelican State. Brown pelicans live at Bayou Sauvage. This endangered bird is the state bird.

GULF OF MEXICO

The National Park Service has seven sites in Louisiana.

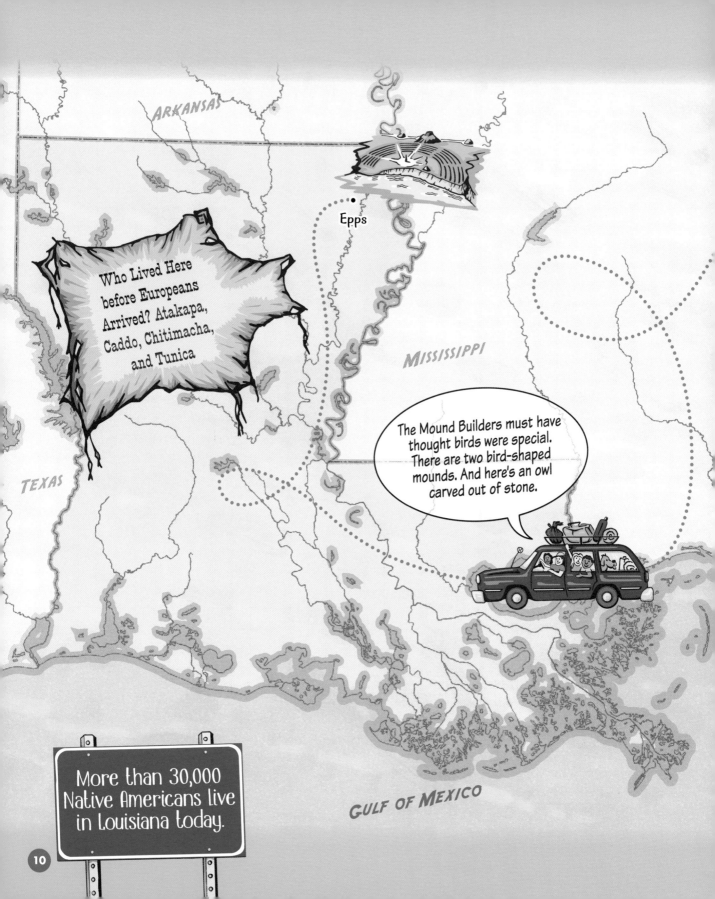

ARKANSAS

Epps

Who Lived Here before Europeans Arrived? Atakapa, Caddo, Chitimacha, and Tunica

MISSISSIPPI

TEXAS

The Mound Builders must have thought birds were special. There are two bird-shaped mounds. And here's an owl carved out of stone.

More than 30,000 Native Americans live in Louisiana today.

GULF OF MEXICO

THE MOUNDS AT POVERTY POINT

Imagine carrying a heavy basket of dirt. Now imagine carrying millions of those baskets! That's what the Mound Builders did at Poverty Point near Epps. The Mound Builders were a group of Native American people. They used the earth to build giant mounds.

One mound is shaped like a bird. Others are long, narrow piles. They stand in a curve, like the letter *C*.

The Mound Builders lived here more than 3,000 years ago. They hunted and fished for food. They also gathered nuts and seeds.

You can walk among the Poverty Point mounds. You can also see things that people made there. There are beads, pots, and spear points. There are also many stone birds.

When viewed from above, Bird Mound at Poverty Point looks like a flying bird.

FORT SAINT JEAN BAPTISTE IN NATCHITOCHES

Log cabins are everywhere at Fort Saint Jean Baptiste. Living-history weekends there are great fun. Everyone's dressed like a French person in the 1700s. Why is that?

French people from Canada explored Louisiana. One was René-Robert Cavelier, Sieur de la Salle. He came down the Mississippi River in 1682. Soon traders and fur trappers arrived. Fort Saint Jean Baptiste was Louisiana's earliest European settlement. A French trader settled it in 1714.

Louisiana passed to Spain and then back to France. The United States bought Louisiana in 1803. This was called the Louisiana Purchase. Steamboats started chugging down the Mississippi River.

See what life was like in a 1700s-era French settlement at Fort Saint Jean Baptiste.

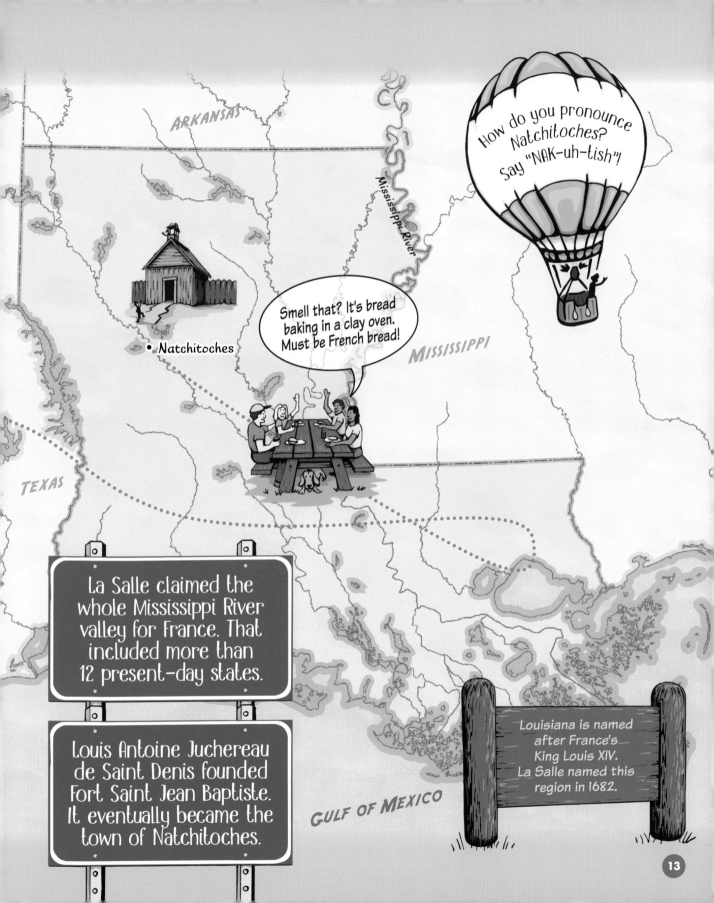

LAFAYETTE'S VERMILIONVILLE

A **blacksmith** hammers out an iron tool. A woman spins cotton at her spinning wheel. A woodworker carves a cypress wood cabinet.

These are daily activities at Vermilionville. This park is like an old Acadian village. Acadians were early settlers in Louisiana.

The first Acadians were French people living in Canada. Their **colony** was called Acadia. British soldiers drove them out in the mid-1700s. Most Acadians settled in southern Louisiana.

In time, the word *Acadian* changed into *Cajun*. Many Cajuns settled in the bayous. They fished, hunted, and farmed. Cajuns developed special food and music. Their language is a form of French. Cajun **culture** is still a big part of life in Louisiana.

Step into Vermilionville's one-room schoolhouse if you want to learn some French.

LOUISIANA FOLKLIFE FESTIVAL IN MONROE

Over there, you might hear ghost stories. Over here, enjoy some **jambalaya**. Here's a fiddler, and there's a mask maker.

You're at the Louisiana Folklife Festival. It offers the best of Louisiana's many **traditions**.

Lots of different **ethnic** groups live in Louisiana. Cajuns and Creoles live in southern Louisiana. Creoles have a mix of backgrounds. Their **ancestors** were African, French, or Spanish settlers.

About one out of three Louisianans is African American. Other people have roots in Hispanic or Asian lands. Each group has special music, foods, crafts, and stories. Come to the festival and enjoy them all!

You'll hear many kinds of music at the Louisiana Folklife Festival.

ARKANSAS

• Shreveport

• Monroe

Let's eat some soul food and listen to ghost stories!

In 2016, 4,681,666 people lived in Louisiana. It's the 25th-largest state by population.

MISSISSIPPI

TEXAS

• Mamou

★ Baton Rouge

• New Orleans

GULF OF MEXICO

Population of Largest Cities

New Orleans...............389,617
Baton Rouge...............228,590
Shreveport..................197,204

Mamou holds the Cajun Music Festival every September.

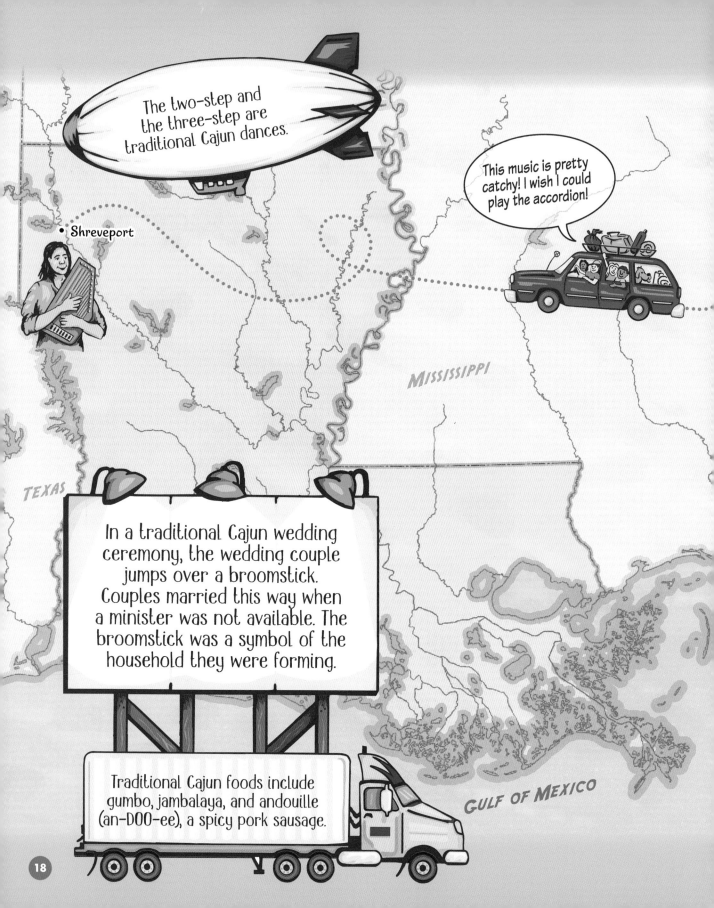

The two-step and the three-step are traditional Cajun dances.

This music is pretty catchy! I wish I could play the accordion!

• Shreveport

MISSISSIPPI

TEXAS

In a traditional Cajun wedding ceremony, the wedding couple jumps over a broomstick. Couples married this way when a minister was not available. The broomstick was a symbol of the household they were forming.

Traditional Cajun foods include gumbo, jambalaya, and andouille (an-DOO-ee), a spicy pork sausage.

GULF OF MEXICO

SHREVEPORT'S MUDBUG MADNESS FESTIVAL

Eat your weight in crawfish. Dance to zydeco music. That's a kind of Creole music. It features guitar, accordion, and fiddle. You're at the Mudbug Madness festival in Shreveport!

Mudbug Madness is a four-day street festival. It is one of Louisiana's most popular music festivals. You'll hear jazz, blues, Cajun, and Creole music. Cajun and Creole music both include instruments such as the accordion and the fiddle. Waltzes are a common type of Cajun music. Creole music has a variety of influences, including the blues and rock and roll.

If you're hungry after dancing, you'll find plenty of Cajun food. Have some red beans and rice. Or maybe you'd like to enter the children's crawfish eating contest. How quickly can you eat 3 pounds (1.4 kilograms) of crawfish?

Listen to some zydeco music at the Mudbug Madness festival.

CONTRABAND DAYS IN LAKE CHARLES

Put on your black eye patch. Paint on some tattoos. Maybe you'll win the pirate costume contest! You're at Lake Charles's Contraband Days festival. It celebrates the days of Jean Lafitte.

Lafitte was a famous pirate. He and his crew attacked ships off Louisiana's coast. They stole the valuable goods onboard. They also sold illegal goods, or contraband.

Lafitte had a good side, too. He helped out in the War of 1812. The United States fought Great Britain in this war.

British soldiers attacked U.S. troops near New Orleans. Lafitte helped General Andrew Jackson win the battle. Then Lafitte became a hero.

Dress in your best pirate garb for Contraband Days in Lake Charles.

Cool! They have helicopter rides!

ARKANSAS

Louisiana was the 18th state to enter the Union. It joined on April 30, 1812.

MISSISSIPPI

TEXAS

Lake Charles

New Orleans •

Chalmette Battlefield and Cemetery is near New Orleans. It's where Jean Lafitte and Andrew Jackson fought in the Battle of New Orleans.

The Battle of New Orleans took place on January 8, 1815. The War of 1812 had ended 15 days earlier. Unfortunately, that information didn't reach New Orleans before the battle.

GULF OF MEXICO

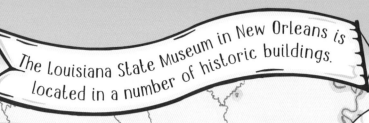

The Louisiana State Museum in New Orleans is located in a number of historic buildings.

You'll find a lot of tasty food in New Orleans. I think I'll try a **beignet**!

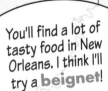

MISSISSIPPI

Dear Mr. Armstrong:
I love hearing you play and sing. "Hello, Dolly" is a great tune. So is "When the Saints Go Marching In." Guess I'd better keep practicing!

Musically yours,
The Scatman Kid

post card

Louis Armstrong
1901-1971
New Orleans, LA

The first public subscription library in Louisiana opened in New Orleans in 1820.

Paul Prudhomme was a famous New Orleans chef. He made Cajun and Creole food.

New Orleans •

Gospel singer Mahalia Jackson (1911-1972) was born in New Orleans. So was jazz pianist Jelly Roll Morton (1890-1941).

Louis Armstrong made scat singing popular. Scat singing uses nonsense words instead of real words.

GULF OF MEXICO

New Orleans Jazz National Historical Park offers a walking tour of 11 sites. Each site is a landmark in jazz history.

ROAMING AROUND NEW ORLEANS

Sniff the air in New Orleans. You'll probably smell something delicious! French pastry shops are everywhere. Lots of restaurants serve Cajun or Creole foods. These foods are famous for being spicy.

New Orleans is a great place to explore. Some sections look like an old European city. The French Quarter was originally built in the 1700s. Its narrow buildings have fancy iron **balconies**.

You're sure to hear music in the air, too. People say jazz was born in New Orleans. Many famous jazz musicians once played there. One was trumpet player Louis Armstrong. He sure could blow that horn!

You're bound to hear some jazz music when you walk the streets of downtown New Orleans.

OAKLAND PLANTATION IN BERMUDA

Y ou are walking on a path shaded by oak trees. Ahead is a wide, white house. In the distance you see a barn and other wooden buildings. You are exploring Oakland **Plantation** in Bermuda.

Oakland Plantation is more than 200 years old. The Spanish government granted Frenchman Jean Pierre Emmanuel Prudhomme the land in 1789. Eight generations of the Prudhomme family lived here. More than 100 enslaved African and Creole people once lived here as well. These enslaved people built the main house and other buildings. They also did much of the labor. Oakland's main crop was cotton.

Enslaved people were freed after the U.S. Civil War (1861–1865). After that, tenant farmers worked the land. These farmers could sell the crops they raised. They then paid rent to the plantation owners.

Oakland Plantation's main house is made of brick and wood from cypress trees.

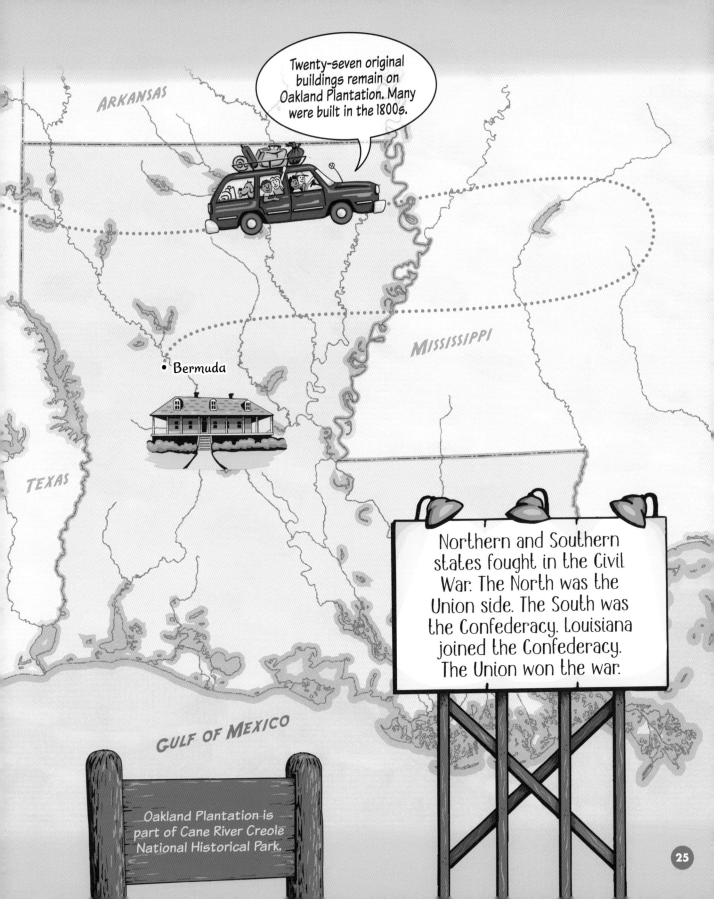

Brown juice is boiling in big kettles. The juice is cane syrup. The kettles are as big as bathtubs!

It's Sugar Day at Kent Plantation. This festival celebrates old-time sugar-making days. Sugar comes from the sugarcane plant. That's still Louisiana's top crop.

How did people turn sugarcane into sugar? First, they pressed juice out of sugarcane stalks. Then they boiled the juice. It became thick, sweet cane syrup. Next, the syrup was dried. This left brown chunks of raw sugar. A few more steps produced white sugar grains. Sugar is made much the same way today. Do you sprinkle sugar on your cereal? You'll have a lot to think about now!

A farmer harvests sugarcane in Louisiana.

OIL CITY'S OIL AND GAS MUSEUM

Oil City was once a pretty wild place. Oil was discovered there in the early 1900s. Soon thousands of people went there to work. Some lived in shacks. They slept on metal beds. Others lived in tents.

Want to learn more about this time period? Just visit Oil City's Oil and Gas Museum!

Oil became a big **industry** in Louisiana. Another big industry began in the 1960s—space! Louisiana began making Saturn rockets. One rocket boosted *Apollo 11* into space in 1969. Its astronauts landed on the Moon!

Learn about Louisiana's oil-boom era at the Oil and Gas Museum.

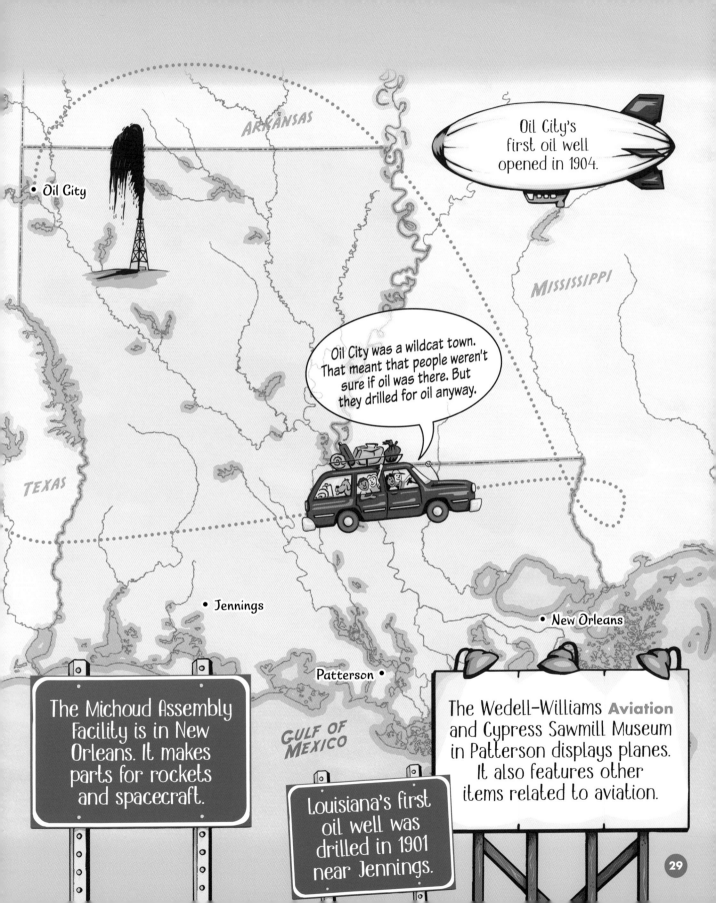

Oil City's first oil well opened in 1904.

Oil City was a wildcat town. That meant that people weren't sure if oil was there. But they drilled for oil anyway.

ARKANSAS

MISSISSIPPI

TEXAS

Oil City

Jennings

New Orleans

Patterson

GULF OF MEXICO

The Michoud Assembly Facility is in New Orleans. It makes parts for rockets and spacecraft.

Louisiana's first oil well was drilled in 1901 near Jennings.

The Wedell-Williams Aviation and Cypress Sawmill Museum in Patterson displays planes. It also features other items related to aviation.

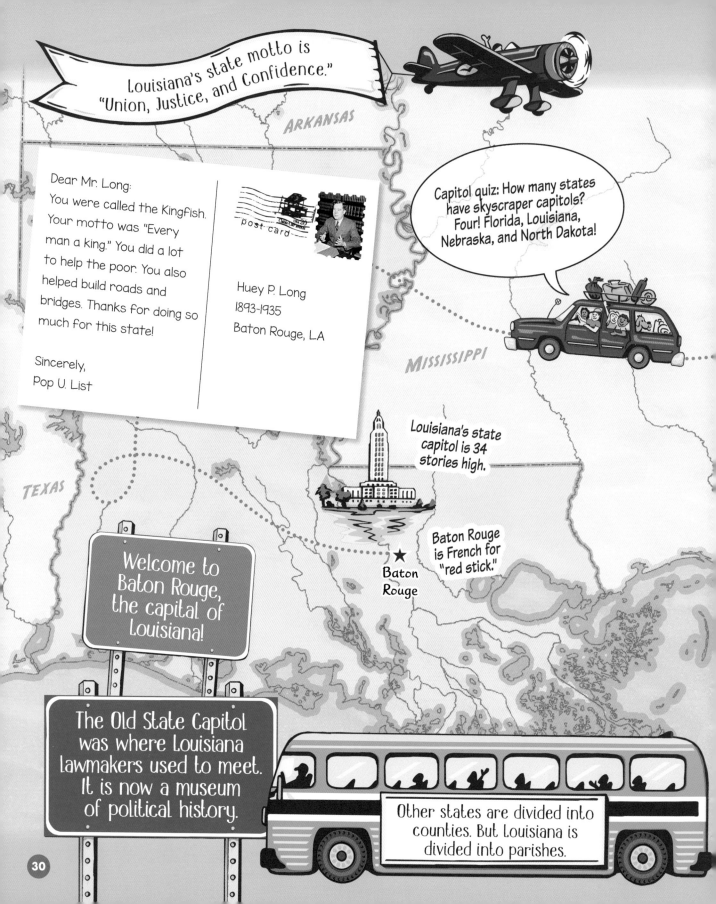

Louisiana's state motto is "Union, Justice, and Confidence."

Dear Mr. Long:
You were called the Kingfish. Your motto was "Every man a king." You did a lot to help the poor. You also helped build roads and bridges. Thanks for doing so much for this state!

Sincerely,
Pop U. List

post card

Huey P. Long
1893-1935
Baton Rouge, LA

Capitol quiz: How many states have skyscraper capitols? Four! Florida, Louisiana, Nebraska, and North Dakota!

ARKANSAS

MISSISSIPPI

TEXAS

Louisiana's state capitol is 34 stories high.

★ Baton Rouge

Baton Rouge is French for "red stick."

Welcome to Baton Rouge, the capital of Louisiana!

The Old State Capitol was where Louisiana lawmakers used to meet. It is now a museum of political history.

Other states are divided into counties. But Louisiana is divided into parishes.

THE STATE CAPITOL IN BATON ROUGE

Stand in front of Louisiana's state capitol. You'll notice something right away. There's no big, curved dome on top. This capitol is a skyscraper. It's the tallest state capitol in the country!

Inside the capitol are state government offices. Louisiana's government is divided into three branches. One branch makes the state's laws. Another branch carries out those laws. It's headed by the governor. The third branch is made up of judges. They decide whether someone has broken a law. Huey Long was a famous Louisiana governor. It was his idea to build the skyscraper capitol.

Climb up to the state capitol's observation deck for a bird's-eye view of Baton Rouge.

Smell the spices. Watch machines whir and blend. Hoppers are dropping tons of beans and rice. They're mixing up Creole and Cajun foods. Once they're ready, meals are packaged up and shipped off. This is Tony Chachere's food plant in Opelousas!

Foods are important factory products in Louisiana. Food factories start out with a farm product. They may clean, boil, chop, or package it. Then it can be sold in stores. Coffee, sugar, and soft drinks are a few examples. So are baked goods and hot sauce.

Louisiana factories also make oil and coal products. Some make medicine, paint, soap, or cardboard. Louisiana builds huge ships, too.

Find out how some spicy Creole food is made at Tony Chachere's food plant.

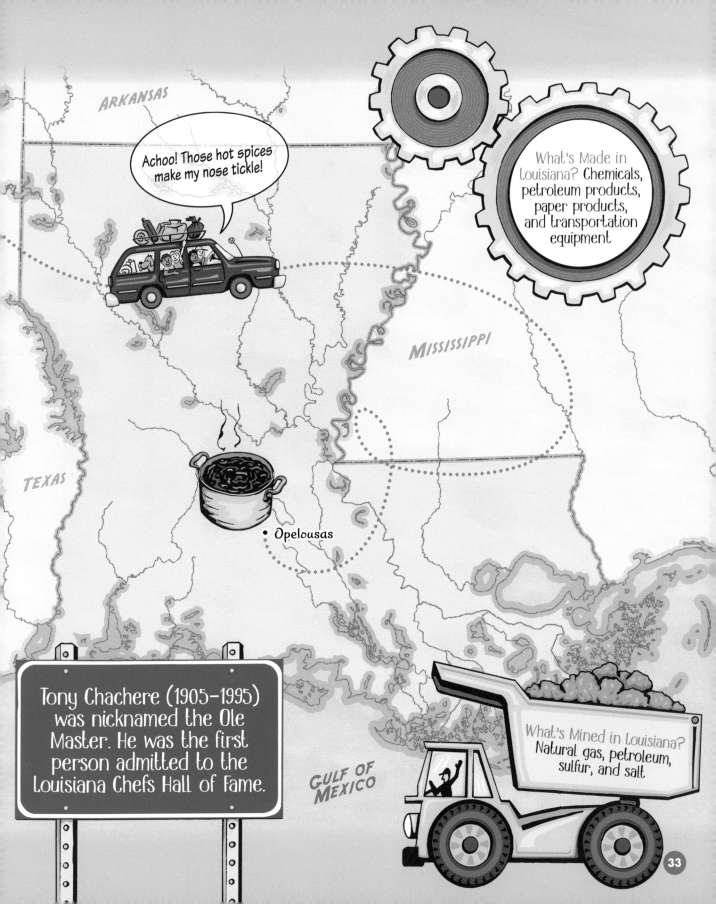

Achoo! Those hot spices make my nose tickle!

What's Made in Louisiana? Chemicals, petroleum products, paper products, and transportation equipment

• Opelousas

Tony Chachere (1905–1995) was nicknamed the Ole Master. He was the first person admitted to the Louisiana Chefs Hall of Fame.

What's Mined in Louisiana? Natural gas, petroleum, sulfur, and salt

The Independence Bowl football game is in Shreveport every year.

The Sugar Bowl is a college football game. It takes place around New Year's Day in New Orleans.

Look at that outfit! I want to dress up as the Mardi Gras queen!

Louisiana Sports Teams
New Orleans Pelicans
(basketball)
New Orleans Saints
(football)

ARKANSAS

MISSISSIPPI

TEXAS

• Shreveport

GULF OF MEXICO

New Orleans •

Mardi Gras is French for "Fat Tuesday." That's the day before Lent begins. Lent is a traditional Christian season before Easter.

The Mercedes-Benz Superdome is a huge stadium in New Orleans. The New Orleans Saints play there. The New Orleans Pelicans play in the Smoothie King Center. It's next to the superdome.

MARDI GRAS WORLD IN NEW ORLEANS

Everywhere you look, there's something big and shiny. Here's a sea monster and a fierce alligator. There's a giant **jester** with bells on his hat.

You're at Mardi Gras World in New Orleans. It's sort of like a factory. It makes decorations for the city's biggest event.

Mardi Gras is a huge carnival. People wear costumes and dance in the streets. Parades with giant floats go by. Each float may have a fancy king or queen. They throw bead necklaces to the crowds. The streets get pretty crowded during Mardi Gras. Everyone is bumping into each other! That's why it's fun to visit Mardi Gras World. You can enjoy the awesome sights in peace!

You'll see many colorful and creative decorations at Mardi Gras World.

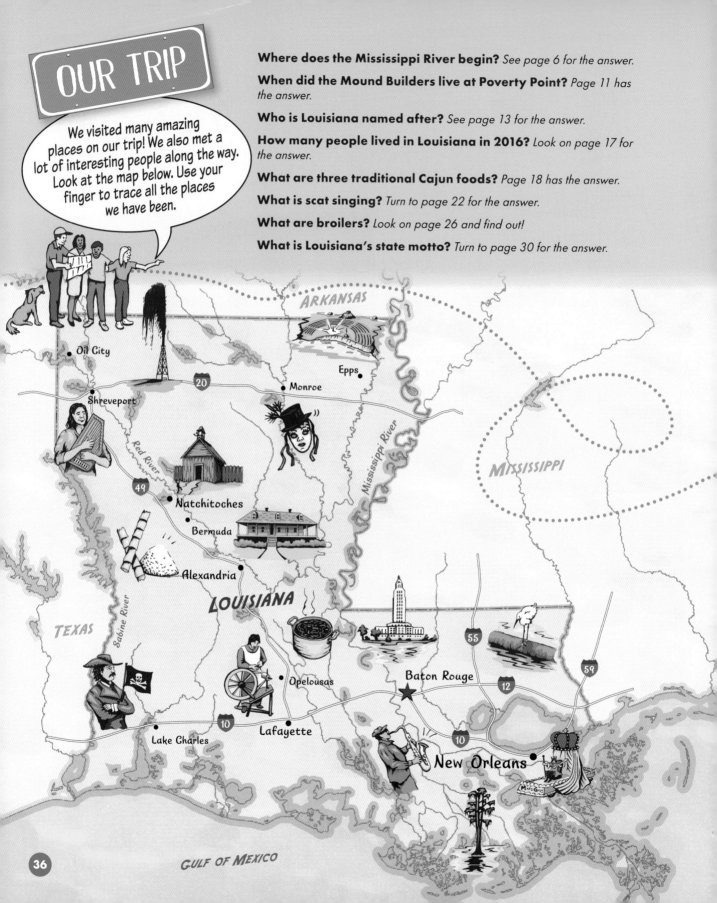

OUR TRIP

We visited many amazing places on our trip! We also met a lot of interesting people along the way. Look at the map below. Use your finger to trace all the places we have been.

Where does the Mississippi River begin? *See page 6 for the answer.*

When did the Mound Builders live at Poverty Point? *Page 11 has the answer.*

Who is Louisiana named after? *See page 13 for the answer.*

How many people lived in Louisiana in 2016? *Look on page 17 for the answer.*

What are three traditional Cajun foods? *Page 18 has the answer.*

What is scat singing? *Turn to page 22 for the answer.*

What are broilers? *Look on page 26 and find out!*

What is Louisiana's state motto? *Turn to page 30 for the answer.*

ARKANSAS

Oil City

Epps

20

Monroe

Shreveport

Red River

49

Natchitoches

MISSISSIPPI

Mississippi River

Bermuda

Alexandria

LOUISIANA

TEXAS

Sabine River

55

59

Baton Rouge

12

Opelousas

10

Lake Charles

Lafayette

10

New Orleans

GULF OF MEXICO

State seal

State flag

STATE SYMBOLS

State amphibian: Green tree frog

State bird: Eastern brown pelican

State colors: Blue, white, and gold

State crustacean: Crawfish

State dog: Catahoula leopard dog

State drink: Milk

State flower: Magnolia

State fossil: Petrified palmwood

State freshwater fish: White perch

State gemstone: Cabochon cut oyster shell

State insect: Honeybee

State mammal: Louisiana black bear

State musical instrument: Diatonic accordion (Cajun accordion)

State reptile: Alligator

State tree: Bald cypress

State wildflower: Louisiana iris

STATE SONG

"GIVE ME LOUISIANA"
Words and music by Doralice Fontane

Give me Louisiana,
The state where I was born
The state of snowy cotton,
The best I've ever known;
A state of sweet magnolias,
And creole melodies
Oh give me Louisiana,
The state where I was born
Oh what sweet old memories
The mossy old oaks bring
It brings us the story of our Evangeline
A state of old tradition,
Of old plantation days
Makes good old Louisiana
The sweetest of all states.

Give me Louisiana,
A state prepared to share
That good old southern custom,
Hospitality so rare;
A state of fruit and flowers,
Of sunshine and spring showers
Oh give me Louisiana,
The state where I was born.

Its woodlands, its marshes
Where humble trappers live
Its rivers, its valleys,
A place to always give
A state where work is pleasure,
With blessings in full measure
Makes good old Louisiana
The dearest of all states.

Give me Louisiana,
Where love birds always sing
In shady lanes or pastures,
The cowbells softly ring;
The softness of the sunset
Brings peace and blissful rest
Oh give me Louisiana,
The state where I was born.
The smell of sweet clover
Which blossoms everywhere
The fresh new mown hay
Where children romp and play
A state of love and laughter,
A state for all here after
Makes good old Louisiana
The grandest of all states.

That was a great trip! We have traveled all over Louisiana! There are a few places that we didn't have time for, though. Next time, we plan to visit the Bayou Pierre Alligator Park in Nachitoches. Visitors can watch the alligators being fed. They can also see alligator training in the swamp.

FAMOUS PEOPLE

Adkins, Trace (1962–), country singer

Armstrong, Louis (1901–1971), musician and singer

Audubon, John James (1785–1851), naturalist and artist

Bradshaw, Terry (1948–), football commentator

Capote, Truman (1924–1984), author

Chopin, Kate (1850–1904), author

Connick Jr., Harry (1967–), singer

DeGeneres, Ellen (1958–), comedian and talk show host

Domino, Fats (1928–), singer

Hellman, Lillian (1905–1984), playwright

Jackson, Mahalia (1911–1972), singer

Manning, Peyton (1976–), football player

Marsalis, Wynton (1961–), trumpet player

McGraw, Tim (1967–), country singer

Morton, Jelly Roll (1890–1941), jazz musician

Newton, Huey P. (1942–1989), political activist

Roberts, Cokie (1943–), journalist

Saxon, Elizabeth Lyle (1832–1915), women's rights activist

Spears, Britney (1981–), singer

Taylor, Zachary (1784–1850), 12th U.S. president

White, Edward Douglass (1845–1921), U.S. Supreme Court justice

Witherspoon, Reese (1976–), actor

WORDS TO KNOW

ancestors (AN-sess-turz) parents, grandparents, great-grandparents, and so on

aviation (ay-vee-AY-shuhn) building and flying airplanes

balconies (BAL-kuh-neez) platforms that stick out from a building and have railings

beignet (behn-YAY) a square doughnut with no hole

blacksmith (BLAK-smith) someone who makes metal objects using fire to heat the metal and a hammer to shape it

colony (KOL-uh-nee) a new land with ties to a parent country

culture (KUHL-chur) a group's customs, beliefs, and way of life

ethnic (ETH-nik) having to do with a person's race or nationality

gumbo (GUHM-boh) thick soup made with okra, a gooey vegetable

industry (IN-duh-stree) a type of business

jambalaya (jum-buh-LYE-uh) spicy stew with rice, meat, and vegetables

jester (JES-tur) a person in a funny suit whose job is to entertain kings and queens

plantation (plan-TAY-shuhn) a large farm that raises mainly one crop

traditions (truh-DISH-uhnz) customs handed down from generation to generation

TO LEARN MORE

IN THE LIBRARY
Felix, Rebecca. *The Southeast*. Mankato, MN: The Child's World, 2014.

Lynette, Rachel. *The Louisiana Purchase*. New York, NY: PowerKids, 2014.

Owings, Lisa. *Louisiana*. Minneapolis, MN: Bellwether, 2014.

Tracy, Kathleen. *Louisiana Creole & Cajun Cultures in Perspective*. Hockessin, DE: Mitchell Lane, 2014.

ON THE WEB
Visit our Web site for links about Louisiana:
childsworld.com/links

*Note to Parents, Teachers, and Librarians: We routinely verify our Web links to make sure
they are safe and active sites. So encourage your readers to check them out!*

PLACES TO VISIT OR CONTACT
Louisiana Office of Tourism
louisianatravel.com
PO Box 94291
Baton Rouge, LA 70804
800/677-4082
For more information about traveling in Louisiana

Louisiana State Museum
louisianastatemuseum.org
PO Box 2448
New Orleans, LA 70176
504/568-6968
For more information about the history of Louisiana

Louisiana covers 52,378 square miles (135,658 sq km). It's the 31st-largest state in size.

INDEX

Bye, Pelican State.
We had a great time.
We'll come back soon!